The Book of
CLASSIC TRAINS

The Book of
CLASSIC TRAINS

Elizabeth Cameron

Illustrated by George J. Zaffo

Mud Puddle inc.
NEW YORK

The Book of Classic Trains • Text by Elizabeth Cameron • Illustrations by George J. Zaffo
This edition published in 2006 by Mud Puddle, Inc., 36 W. 25th Street, New York, NY 10010, USA • info@mudpuddleinc.com
Originally published as The Big Book of Real Trains by Grosset & Dunlap Publishers • New York
Copyright © 1949, 1953, 1963 by Grosset & Dunlap Publishers
ISBN: 1-59412-121-4

Printed in China, May 2019

1 3 5 7 9 10 8 6 4 2

THE LOCOMOTIVE AND TENDER • The engine comes out of the roundhouse. It is cleaned and oiled. The tender behind the engine carries coal and water. The locomotive is ready for a trip. This locomotive has four pilot wheels in front. These keep the engine on the track. It has six driving wheels. These make the engine go. Four other wheels carry the back of the engine.

HOPPER • A steel hopper car carries coal and gravel. It also carries different kinds of ore. A hopper is loaded from the top. It is loaded by an automatic loader. A switch engine moves the hopper under the loading bin. The coal or gravel goes through the chutes into the hopper.

COVERED HOPPER • The covered hopper has a roof over the top. There are eight hatches on the roof. The hatches are opened to load the hopper. The covered hopper carries sugar, cement or grain. No moisture can get in to harden the hopper's cargo.

SUPER FLATCAR • The super flat car has thirty two wheels. The center of the super flat car is depressed. Huge heavy machinery or electric transformers are carries in the depressed center. The center is depressed so that the car can go under bridges with its cargo.

FLATCAR • A flat car is a platform on wheels. It has no top or walls. It has stakes instead along the sides. The stakes keep the cargo in the flat car from falling off. Flat cars can haul large pieces of machinery. They also haul huge logs and boards from the sawmills. Sometimes big tractors are carried on a flat car.

CATTLE CAR • This livestock car carries cattle. It has one deck. It has slits on each side to let in fresh air for the animals. Some livestock cars carry sheep and pigs. They have two decks. Cars that carry chickens and turkeys have many decks. Animals cannot travel more than a day and a half in a freight car. This is the law. The cattle cars stop at resting places. The animals have food and water in the resting pens. They have time to exercise, too.

PIGGY-BACK CAR • The piggy-back car carries trailer boxes. Some
piggy-back cars carry one trailer box. Others carry two. Some trains are made
up only of piggy-back cars. These trains travel mostly at night. The trailer box is
secured to the deck of the piggy-back car. Jacks are placed under the box. The
jacks hold the body of the trailer box up, in case the box gets a flat tire.

AUTO CAR • The auto car carries new cars from the factory. It carries them to all parts of the country. Each auto car carries nine standard-size cars. The auto car can carry fifteen compact cars. Automobiles ride safely in the auto car.

THE GONDOLA • The

gondola is a metal box on wheels.
It has no top. It carries things
that snow and rain cannot hurt. It
is loaded and unloaded by men.
Sometimes the men use machines
to load the car.

Gondolas haul pieces of
machinery. They haul pipes,
cement blocks, steel plates and
other things.

THE REFRIGERATOR CAR •

A refrigerator car carries fruits and vegetables. It carries meat and fish. It carries butter and eggs. It even carries fresh flowers.

Men fit canvas funnels over the doors. Machines blow cold air into the car. Then the car is loaded. The doors are closed. Ice is put in at each end of the refrigerator car. More ice is put in at stations along the way.

MECHANICAL REFRIGERATOR CAR • The mechanical refrigerator car carries its own refrigerator. The refrigerator is run by diesel fuel. The temperature in the car can be kept at 70°, or as low as 10° below zero. A mechanical refrigerator car carries fresh fruits and vegetables. It can also carry frozen foods.

DOUBLE-DOOR BOX CAR •

The double-door on the boxcar makes it easy to load and unload large cargo. The box car carries dry goods that are packed in boxes. It carries barrels and bales. It carries bundles and bags. It even carries small boats. The box car is made of metal in the outside and lined with wood on the inside.

NP

NP 7104
CAPY. 100000   XM
LD LMT. 113100
LT. WT. 55900

ROUTE OF THE
VISTA-DOME
NORTH COAST
LIMITED

NORTHERN PACIFIC RAILWAY

TANK CAR • Tank cars are really big cans with different kinds of linings. Milk tank cars have glass or steel linings. Cars that carry chemicals are lined with rubber, lead or aluminum. Tank cars have one or more domes on top. In warm weather the liquid expands and goes up the dome. If liquid could not expand, the car might break at the seams. There are more than 200 different kinds of tank cars.

S.C.C.X 151

CAPY. 100000 LBS.
LT. WT. 44 T

CABOOSE • The caboose is the last car of the train. It is an office, a bedroom, and a kitchen. The rear breakman sits in the place on top and watches the whole train. On long trips the train crew cooks dinner in the caboose. The caboose has a telephone. The crew can talk to the engineer and the fireman up front.

CLASSIFICATION YARD • The classification yard is where you can see all kinds of freight cars. New trains are made up at one end of the yard. Incoming trains are "cut" at the classification yard. Cars that are to remain at this yard for unloading or loading are put on certain tracks. Cars that are to go on to the next terminal are put on other tracks. The train that is being cut is at the highest point of the yard. This is called the "hump". As each car (or group of cars) is cut, it coasts downhill. Men in the two towers control the retarders. The retarders act as brakes on the coasting cars. The cars are made to slow up just enough so that they won't bang into the parked cards on the track that they are approaching.

DIESEL SWITCHER • The diesel switch engine is the work horse of the yard. It is used to push or pull the many freight cars in the yard. The switch engine is used to make up a new train. It is used to move new cards to different sidings in the yard. This diesel switch engine has the power to pull about forty-five freight cars. Railroad men call the switch engine a "drill" engine.

PARTS OF A LOCOMOTIVE

1. **Water Tank.**
2. **Stoker.** Coal is carried to the stoker. Steam jets blow it to all parts of the fire bed.
3. **Throttle Lever.**
4. **Water Gauge.** It shows how much water is in the boiler. Water must always cover the crown sheet. (See 5.)
5. **Crown Sheet.** Moist steam is blown over the crown sheet. This is the hottest part of the firebox.
6. **Steam.**
7. **Water.**
8. **Safety Valve.** It opens to keep the steam pressure from getting to high.
9. **Throttle Valve.** It controls steam that runs locomotive.
10. **Dry Pipe.** It carries steam to the valve and cylinders. (See 18 and 19.)
11. **Bell.** It rings by air pressure.
12. **Water Delivery Pipe.** (See 22.)
13. **Sand Dome.** Sand is blown down the sand pipes if the track is slippery. (See 14.)

14. **Sand Pipe.**
15. **Superheater Tubes.**
16. **Smokebox.** It is filled with exhaust gases.
17. **Valve Piston.** It guides steam in and out of the cylinder.

18. **Valve.**
19. **Cylinder.**
20. **Coal Bunker.**
21. **Worm Coal Conveyer.**
22. **Injector.** Water comes from the tender to the injector. It mixes

30. Side Rod. It takes power from the main rod to both large wheels.

31. Radius Rod. It controls the engine going forward and going backward. The radius rod is lifted up when the engine goes the other way.

32. Valve Gear. It controls the going up or going down of the radius rod.

33. Sand Pipe Outlet.

34. Crosshead. It is the place where the main rod joins the piston.

with a jet of steam. The steam and water push their way up the delivery pipe and into the boiler.

23. Reverse Lever.

24. Grate.

25. Brick Arch.

26. Ashpam Hopper. It lets out ashes from the grate. (See 24.)

27. Eccentric Crank.

28. Eccentric Rod.

29. Main Rod. It gets its power from the piston. (See 35.)

35. Piston. Steam comes in from the right through the dry pipe and pushes the piston to the left. This pushes the main rod and makes the engine go.

TRAIN SIGNALS

WHISTLE SIGNALS

 A SERIES OF SHORT TOOTS
Alarm for persons or animals on track.

 3 SHORT TOOTS
A. Back up (when train is still).
B. Stop at next station (when running).

 1 SHORT TOOT
Stop.

 1 SHORT • 1 LONG TOOT
Brakes sticking, or inspect train line for leak

 2 LONG TOOTS
Release breaks and go ahead.

 1 LONG • 3 SHORT TOOTS
Flagman, guard rear of train.

 1 LONG TOOT
Approaching station, rail crossing, or tunnel.

AIR SIGNAL CORD

 2 PULLS ON CORD
A. Start (when train is still).
B. Stop at once (when running).

 3 PULLS ON CORD
A. Back train (when still).
B. Stop at next passenger station (when running).

LANTERN SIGNALS

 STOP
Swing back and forth across track

REDUCE SPEED
Held at arms length

 PROCEED
Raised and lowered

TRAIN PARTED
Swing in circle at arm's length across tracks

 APPLY AIR BRAKES
Swing above head

RELEASE AIR BRAKES
Held at arm's length above the head

EMERGENCY STOP SIGNALS

WHAT MAKES A STREAMLINED LOCOMOTIVE RUN

This is Unit "A" of a two unit locomotive. Unit "A" contains the cab where the engineer and the fireman sit.

KEY TO NUMBERS

1. Headlight
2. Control Unit
3. Engineer's Seat
4. Cab
5. Horn
6. Electrical Cabinets
7. Ventilation Hatch
8. Traction Motor Blower
9. Fuel Injectors
10. Cooling System (A.C. Motor Driven Fans)
11. 12 Cylinder Diesel Engine (1125 h.p.). There are two engines in this unit, making a total of 2250 h.p.
12. Oil Cooler
13. Dynamic Brakers
14. Outer Shell of Locomotive. The other 112 h.p., engine is inside.
15. Separate Steam Genrator Room

16. Coupler
17. Toilet
18. Brake Cylinder
19. Springs
20. Brake Shoes
21. Sand Pipe
22. Main Air Reservoirs
23. WaterCooled Air Compressor
24. Combination Fuel and Water Tank: 1200 gals. of fuel, 1350 gals. of water
25. Main Air Reservoirs
26. Traction Motor
27. Blower, for Traction Motor
28. Main Generator
29. Steps
30. Air Brake Equipment
31. Pilot

THE MEN WHO RUN THE TRAINS

A crew of 38 men is required to perform the many services for safe, comfrotable and convenient travel aboard a streamliner like the Pennsylvania Railroad's Congressional Limited. This drawing shows where each man is assigned.

1. **Conductor:** Captain of the train, his word is law. He watches over the welfare of the passengers and crew.

2. **Trainmen:** Two men who help collect tickets and aid conductor in safe operation of the train.

3. **Engineer:** Head man in the cab, who runs the locomotive and is responsible for its speeds, signals and safety.

4. **Fireman:** Second man in the cab, who helps the engineer check the road signals and other safety measures.

5. **Pullman Conductors:** Two "lieutenants" under the conductor, who collect reservations for Pullman space.

6. **Porter:** Every sleeping car and Pullman chair car has a porter who helps to make the passengers comfortable.

7. **Stewards:** Two men in charge of dining and kitchen cars. They order supplies and provide for seating and comfort of guests.

8. **Chef:** Top man in the kitchen, he has charge of the proper prepration of the food.

9. **Cooks:** Three men who assist the chef in preparing the meals and menus of the day.

10. **Pantryman:** The "middle-man" between the kitchen crew and the waiters. He watches over the niceties of customer service.

11. **Waiters:** Eight men who serve the guests.

A. **Kitchen-Lounge:** Half of the car is the kitchen where all the food is prepared. The other half is a lounge where beverages are served.

B. **Full-Length Diner:** The restaurant on the train.